# Wreckage

## Tom Ratcliffe

T0353258

*methuen* | drama

LONDON • NEW YORK • OXFORD • NEW DELHI • SYDNEY

METHUEN DRAMA
Bloomsbury Publishing Plc
50 Bedford Square, London, WC1B 3DP, UK
1385 Broadway, New York, NY 10018, USA
29 Earlsfort Terrace, Dublin 2, Ireland

BLOOMSBURY, METHUEN DRAMA and the Methuen
Drama logo are trademarks of Bloomsbury Publishing Plc

First published in Great Britain 2022

Cover design by Jade Barnett

Cover photograph by Darius Shu

A catalogue record for this book is available from the British Library.

Library of Congress Control Number: 2022941857

ISBN: PB: 978-1-3503-5799-0
ePDF: 978-1-3503-5800-3
eBook: 978-1-3503-5801-0

Series: Modern Plays

Typeset by Mark Heslington Ltd, Scarborough, North Yorkshire

To find out more about our authors and books visit
www.bloomsbury.com and sign up for our newsletters.

# Tom Ratcliffe – Writer/Actor

Tom is an award-winning, internationally produced writer / actor and is Co-Executive Director of Wildcard. Writing credits include: *Evelyn* (Southwark Playhouse / Mercury Theatre), *VELVET* (UK and Ireland tour / Pleasance Courtyard), *Circa* (Theater de Meervaart, Amsterdam / The Old Red Lion) and *Gifted* (Pleasance Theatre). Tom was awarded the JB Priestley Award for Writers of Promise in 2020. He was shortlisted for the Old Vic 12 in 2016 and has been longlisted for the Verity Bargate, Theatre503 and Papatango playwriting awards. Short plays have included runs at Theatre503, Old Red Lion Theatre and St James Theatre.

Acting credits include: *VELVET* (UK and Ireland tour / Pleasance Courtyard), *Sket* (Park Theatre), *5 Guys Chillin'* (King's Head Theatre / Assembly Roxy) and *Wars of the Roses* (Rose Theatre, Kingston). Film credits include *Once Upon a Time in London* (Gateway Films).

# Michael Walter – Actor

Theatre includes: *Steve* (Seven Dials Playhouse), *The Inheritance* (Young Vic and West End transfer), *Death of a Salesman* (Royal and Derngate / UK tour), *If You Kiss Me, Kiss Me* (Young Vic), *In the Jungle of Cities* (Arcola Theatre) and *Anna Christie* (Donmar Warehouse).

Television and film includes: *The Sandman*, *Now You See Me 2*, *About Time*.

# Rikki Beadle-Blair MBE – Director

Rikki Beadle-Blair MBE is a writer, director, composer, choreographer, designer, producer and performer. He has won several awards including the Sony Award, the Los Angeles Outfest Screenwriting and Outstanding Achievement awards. Every year he hosts UK Black Pride,

Manchester Black Pride, plus annual Vogue balls in Manchester, Liverpool, Birmingham, Leeds and other cities around the UK. In 2016 he was made an MBE (Member of the British Empire) by HRH Queen Elizabeth II. His projects include several feature films and TV series, including *Blackbird*, starring Oscar-winning actress, Mo'nique, *Stonewall* for the BBC, *Metrosexuality* for Channel 4, *Noah's Arc* for MTV LOGO as well as *FIT, KickOff* and *Bashment* for his own company Team Angelica. He is one of the creative directors of the Visionary Youth Project for young European Film Activists. Rikki also works extensively in theatre and has written forty plays in the last twenty years that have been performed at Theatre Royal Stratford East, the Bush Theatre, the Soho Theatre, the Tristan Bates Theatre and the Contact Theatre in Manchester. Rikki is committed mentor to a great many writers, actors, composers and directors.

## Rory Davies – Producer

Rory has been the Artistic and Executive Director at Harlow Playhouse since 2017. Prior to this he worked in general management and toured the UK as a production manager. As a freelancer, he also worked as an Event Manager, Electrical Technician and Stage Manager. Rory has also been the Technical Director of Nationally Honoured inclusive theatre company Razed Roof.

Rory has been responsible for producing a number of family shows, including pantomime, at and for Harlow Playhouse and on tour. In the subsidised sector Rory has commissioned *I Talk to the Clouds* and *They Cry with Me* by Rhiannon Faith, *Wreckage* by Tom Ratcliffe and has co-produced a number of shows including *Prom Kween*, *With One Look* and *Drowntown*. Rory is enthusiastic about working with and developing artists and as such has mentored many of Harlow's emerging artists.

Rory has provided management consultancy for various companies including KD Theatre Productions, AC Special

Projects, Passmores Community Learning Trust and numerous pantomime production companies. Rory is a professional member of UK Theatre and is on the Essex Power 100 list, recognising the most influential people in Essex.

Rory is a Trustee for the Livewire Theatre Trust, Governor of The Downs Primary School, Vice-Chair of Essex Police (Harlow) Independent Advisory Group representing Harlow Playhouse and the LGBTQ+ Community, and member of Harlow's Cultural Leaders Group.

## Daniel Bell – Associate Producer

Daniel is Managing Director and Producer for KD Theatre Productions. Daniel is also a freelance Writer, Director, Producer and founder of KD Academy (Performing Arts Academy).

As a Producer, Daniel has produced a variety of work which has toured regional venues across the UK, London and Edinburgh Fringe Festival. Each Christmas, Daniel is responsible for a season of Family Christmas Productions for KD Theatre Productions.

Daniel is an associate producer for Harlow Playhouse, as well as Writer and Director for their Christmas Pantomime since 2015.

## Madison Parker – Assistant Producer

Madison is a Producer and Creative from Harlow, in Essex. She is currently in the final stages of her Masters Degree in Producing at The Royal Central School of Speech and Drama. Madison works independently and with her theatre company The 5 O'Clock Club. She has produced shows which have gone to The Chiswick Playhouse, The Hope Theatre, the Brighton Fringe and the King's Head Theatre.

She is currently part of the 22/23 Cohort of Stage One's 'Bridge The Gap' Programme.

Madison's passion is in storytelling and she hopes the work she creates and produces reflects the stories of the masses.

## Nadine Rennie – Casting Director

Nadine was in-house Casting Director at Soho Theatre for over fifteen years; working on new plays by writers including Dennis Kelly, Bryony Lavery, Arinzé Kene, Roy Williams, Philip Ridley, Laura Wade, Hassan Abdulrazzak, Vicky Jones and Oladipo Agboluaje.

Since going freelance in January 2019, Nadine has worked for theatres across London and the UK including Arcola Theatre, Orange Tree Theatre, Sheffield Crucible, Leeds Playhouse, Fuel Theatre, National Theatre of Wales, Northern Stage, Pleasance Theatre London, Almeida, Lyric Hammersmith, Hampstead Theatre and continues to cast on a regular basis for Soho Theatre. Nadine also has a long-running association as Casting Director for Synergy Theatre Project.

Recent theatre includes: *Evelyn* (Wildcard/Mercury Theatre/Southwark); *Buritannics* (Lyric Hammersmith); *The Breach* (Hampstead Theatre); *The Ministry of Lesbian Affairs* (Soho Theatre); *Bacon* (Finborough Theatre); *He Said She Said* (Synergy Theatre tour); *The Tempest* (Wildcard/Pleasance Theatre).

TV work includes BAFTA-winning CBBC series *Dixi*, casting the first three series. Nadine is a member of the Casting Directors Guild.

## Harlow Playhouse

Harlow is one of the most economically productive and fastest-growing places in the UK. Arts and Culture is significant in Harlow's history, today and in the future.

We provide a programme of quality wide-ranging work across our 400-seat and 120-seat theatres, as well as other reach-out locations, and provide space and support to many artists, groups and companies throughout the year in our three dynamic studio spaces.

Our mission at Harlow Playhouse is to create a vibrant, wide-ranging programme; work with a social conscience, healthy living, positive wellbeing, and provide a platform for participation in the arts.

As a leading cultural hub Harlow Playhouse continues to commission, produce, co-produce, seed-fund and support a number of artists, including Tom Ratcliffe.

Our vision is to be THE CULTURAL HEART OF HARLOW FOR EVERYONE.

Harlow Playhouse wishes to give thanks to our technical operators William Deady and Thomas Sadler

## KD Theatre Productions – General Management

Passionately spearheaded by co-founders Katherine Hickmott and Daniel Bell, KD Theatre Productions has built a strong reputation since its formation in 2013 and presents a variety of high-quality and innovative productions at venues across the UK.

KD Theatre Productions have produced musical productions of *Anything Goes*, *Hello Dolly*, *Fame, Honk!*, as well as a variety of pantomimes and family shows. Since 2019, KD Theatre Productions have produced Ely's Open Air Theatre in the grounds of Ely Cathedral.

KD Theatre Productions also offer theatrical services to other companies and productions, including General Management, Casting and Production Hire.

For more information, please visit www.kdtheatre.co.uk

*For Frida, Bobby and everyone in the sky.*
*This one's for you.*

# Wreckage

## Characters

**Sam**, *male, late twenties*
**Noel**, *male, late thirties*
**Christian**, *male, early thirties*

*The play is set in the grieving mind of* **Sam***.*

**Noel** *and* **Christian** *should be played by the same actor.*

## Notes on Text

*This play is written to be performed on a bare stage.*

*An indented rule indicates a change in* **Sam***'s mind.*

*Pauses and beats are indicated by the space given between lines.*

*/ Indicates that the next line should start and overlap.*

*– Indicates an interruption by the following line.*

*4.28pm. 12 October 2021. The moment.*

*Lights up.*

*At this moment in the play the staging should seem as natural as possible. Time is how we know it to exist. We are in the present. In reality. This is happening, in the flesh, right now.*

**Sam**   Shit

**Noel**   What?

**Sam**   Fuck

**Noel**   What?

**Sam**   Cu –

**Noel**   What?

**Sam**   Urgggggggggggggggh
I'm a knob I'm a knob I'm a knob

**Noel**   Sam?

**Sam**   Why am I such a –

**Noel**   Breathe –

**Sam**   Twat
Bloody

**Noel**   Breathe Sam

**Sam**   Keys
I took them by mistake
There's no keys to open up
Eva needs them to open up

**Noel**   What about the spare –

**Sam**   You know I've already lost those
I'm supposed to put them in the bloody

**Noel**   Lockbox?

**Sam**   I was tired it was late I didn't

**Noel**   Think

**Sam**   I know I'm a mess I'm such a

**Noel**   How long 'til she –

**Sam**   Half an hour

**Noel**   You've got time

**Sam**   I don't have time
I've got so much to do
Fucking research
Reading
I don't understand any of it
There's a reason I didn't go to uni first time around
I couldn't do it at eighteen let alone at
Twenty-five alongside work
An actual job
I get stressed
Confused
I can't breathe
I'm stupid
Stupider with age
I'm a stupid –

**Noel**   Give me the keys

**Sam**   No
You can't

**Noel**   Give me the keys

**Sam**   Are you sure?

**Noel**   Keys

**Sam**   You're working

**Noel**   I'll go in the car
Twenty minutes there and back
Job done
Call it a fag break

**Sam**   You don't smoke

**Noel**   Breathe
Study
You are more than capable
We've got this
As you were

**Sam**   I love you

**Noel**   Shut up
Text me the code

**Sam**   I love you I love you I love you I love you I love you

---

*There is a change. We are no longer in time as we know it. The world isn't as bright. It is dark and jaded. We can make out shapes visually but that is all.*

**Sam** *is on his own. We are in his mind.*

*We can hear a variety of sounds. A dull beep gradually growing in sharpness. The sounds of muffled voices – it's as if people are speaking to* **Sam** *underwater. We hear a crashing sound – the detail of metal crumpling under intense impact. We hear someone screaming underwater. We hear the same crashing sound again, it is louder. We hear it again, it is louder. We hear it again, it is louder. We hear the same scream underwater. We hear slow thumping on glass. We hear the scream again. The beep is as sharp and loud as it can be. It overwhelms everything.*

---

**Sam**   I don't have time
I've got so much to do
Fucking research
Reading
I don't understand any of it
There's a reason I didn't go to uni first time around
I couldn't do it at eighteen let alone at

Twenty-five alongside work
An actual job
I get stressed
Confused
I can't breathe
I'm stupid
Stupider with age
I'm a stupid –

**Noel**    Give me the keys

*Something changes in* **Sam**. *As if he has just become conscious.*
**Noel** *plays the following exactly how he did previously regardless of*
**Sam**'s *change.*

**Sam**    No
I'll go
/ I'll walk down

**Noel**    Give me the keys

**Sam**    I said no
/ It's fine
Go back to –

**Noel**    I'll go in the car
Twenty minutes there and back
Job done
/ I'll say it's a fag break

**Sam**    I SAID NO
Why aren't you listening?

**Noel**    Breathe
Study
You are more than capable
/ We've got this
As you were

**Sam**    Stop it

**Noel**    / Shut up
Text me the code

**Sam**   STOP IT
STOP

---

**Sam** *is on his own.*

*We hear a crashing sound – the detail of metal crumpling under
intense impact. We hear someone screaming underwater. We hear the
same crashing sound again, it is louder. We hear it again, it is louder.*

---

**Sam**   I'm stupid
Stupider with age
I'm a stupid –

**Noel**   Give me the keys

**Sam**   Don't go

**Noel**   Give me the keys

**Sam**   Please don't go

**Noel**   Keys

---

**Sam** *is on his own.*

*We hear a crashing sound – the detail of metal crumpling under
intense impact. We hear someone screaming underwater. We hear the
same crashing sound again, it is louder. We hear it again, it is louder.*

---

**Noel**   Breathe
/ Study
You are more than capable
We've got this
As you were

**Sam**   No no no no no no no no no no no no no no / no

**Noel**    Shut up
/ Text me the code

**Sam**    No no no no no no no no

---

**Sam** *is on his own.*

*We hear a crashing sound – the detail of metal crumpling under intense impact. We hear someone screaming underwater. We hear the same crashing sound again, it is louder. We hear it again, it is louder.*

---

**Noel**    Text me the code

**Sam**    I love you I love you I love you I love you I love you

---

**Noel** *is lying on the floor. He is not moving.*

**Sam** *is standing over him. He picks up a clear bag of* **Noel**'s *belongings. It contains the keys we saw him give to* **Noel**.

*This sight is destroying him.*

---

**Noel**    Hey

**Sam**    Hello basic carbonara man

**Noel**    You can call me Noel

**Sam**    Can I?

**Noel**    Absolutely

**Sam**    Friends stood you up?

**Noel**    No

**Sam**    You sure about that?

**Noel**    Yep
Just me tonight

**Sam**    That's a large table for one

**Noel**    I always sit there

**Sam**    You always have friends

**Noel**    I like that table
I always have great service

**Sam**    Is that so?

**Noel**    Absolutely

**Sam**    Well done me

**Noel**    Well done you

**Sam**    You're a stickler for routine

**Noel**    Am I?

**Sam**    Same dish
Same table

**Noel**    I know what I like

**Sam**    A man of simple pleasures

**Noel**    Nothing wrong with simple
People should embrace what is simple more often

**Sam**    Have you come over here to give me profound life advice?

**Noel**    No –

**Sam**    Live laugh love?

**Noel**    I'm actually on my way to the gents

**Sam**    That's funny
They're right by your table

**Noel**    So they are
That is funny

**Sam**

**Noel**   You're cute

**Sam**   Bold

**Noel**   You are

**Sam**   And you're 'old enough to be my dad'

**Noel**   I'm sorry?

**Sam**   That's what your friend said
Last time you were here

**Noel**   You heard that?

**Sam**   Yep

**Noel**   That's embarrassing

**Sam**   It is a bit

**Noel**   He saw us flirting

**Sam**   I don't flirt on the job
I'm a professional

**Noel**   Is that so?

**Sam**   Was he lying?

**Noel**   About my age?

**Sam**   Are you old enough to be my dad?

**Noel**   Rude

**Sam**   Are you?

**Noel**   Perhaps?

**Sam**   Perhaps?

**Noel**   If I fucked your mum when I was ten

**Sam**   Did you?

**Noel**   Absolutely

**Sam**   So are you gonna leave your number on a napkin?
Hope I rush to clear the table?
Get there first

**Noel**   Is that how it usually goes?

**Sam**   Leave a good tip?

**Noel**   I don't pay people to date me

**Sam**   I don't suppose you do

You want to date me?

**Noel**   I'd like to take you on a date

Would you like to go on a date?

---

**Noel**   'Sweden
Sweden'

**Sam**   Shut up
They were shit

**Noel**   'Sweden
Sweden'

**Sam**   Why are you chanting like a neanderthal

**Noel**   'Sweden/
Sweden'

**Sam**   It's Eurovision not the World Cup

**Noel**   'Sweden
Sweden'

**Sam**   One more time and you're going in the canal

**Noel**   Really?

**Sam**   Yeah

**Noel**    You would do that to me?

**Sam**    Absolutely
Wouldn't think twice

**Noel**    You're cold

**Sam**    You will be

**Noel**    'Swe –

**Sam** *shoves* **Noel**.

Did you just try to push me in?

**Sam**    God are you always this annoying?

**Noel**    HELP
HELP

**Sam**    Shut –

**Noel**    THIS BOY IS TRYING TO KILL ME

**Sam**    Wait
Boy?

**Noel**    Where's the lie?

**Sam**    Alright daddy

**Noel** *puts his arms around* **Sam**.

**Noel**    I love London at night
All the lights
The bustle
The people

**Sam**    Why don't you live here?

**Noel**    I don't need to
I can come here for work
Enjoy the city
Go home
I don't need to be surrounded by it all the time

**Sam**    You're a regional man

**Noel**    I'm a family man
What can I say?
Home is where the heart is

**Sam**    Christ I couldn't wait to get away from mine

**Noel**    That's sad

Life's all about the connections you make
Why would I want to live away from the people that matter most?
That just doesn't make sense to me

**Sam**

**Noel**    What?

**Sam**    Nothing

**Noel**    I'll get you up to Cambridge before long

**Sam**    To visit maybe

**Noel**    Who knows

**Sam**    God I could never
Cambridge
What zone even is that?

**Noel** *laughs.*

**Noel**    We'll see

**Sam**    It's never gonna happen
Trust me

**Noel**    I already trust you


Hi

*They are close. It is intimate.*

Wait
I need to pee

**Sam**    Okay

**Noel**    Hold that thought
I don't want to be
You know
Desperate
Wishing away our first kiss

**Sam**    Who says I was going to kiss you?

**Noel**    Stand guard

**Sam**    You're gonna pee here?

**Noel**    It's dark

**Sam**    So?
There are still people

**Noel**    I'm counting on you

**Noel** *steps aside.*

**Sam** *stands feeling awkward. Whilst he's not being watched he can't help but smile. He is enjoying the date.*


**Sam**    My god

**Noel**    Two secs


**Noel** *is back. The pair are close.*

**Noel**    Where were we?

**Sam**    You tell me

*They kiss.*

---

**Sam** *is on his own. Lights flickers off* **Sam***'s skin giving the effect of videos projected on him, the images running through his mind.*

*We can hear a voice note from* **Noel** *to* **Sam**. **Sam** *plays it again.*
*Another voice note overlaps. This continues to build until there is a*
*cacophony of voice notes playing at once.*

**Sam** *is in a trance.*

---

**Sam** *is on his own on stage. We cannot see* **Noel**, *only hear his*
*voice.*

**Sam**   It's really you

**Noel**   It's really me

**Sam**   Your voice

**Noel**   No shit

**Sam**   No

**Noel**   What?

**Sam**   I've lost it
Completely bloody

**Noel**   You haven't

**Sam**   This isn't normal

**Noel**   What is normal these days?

**Sam**   See

**Noel**   What?

**Sam**   You wouldn't say that
Noel wouldn't say that

**Noel**   What would I say?

**Sam**   You're not real you're some
Thing some
Healing
Coping mechanism my brain's inventing

**Noel**   Is it working?

**Sam**   What?

**Noel**   I hope it's working

**Sam**   Stop it

**Noel**   I'm worried about you

**Sam**   Fuck it
Why not go completely fucking loopy

Come on then
Appear

Come on

**Noel**   Sam

**Sam**   I can't picture you
I
Why can't I see you?

**Noel**   If you could see me
Right now
What would you do?

**Sam** *smiles.*

There we go
Haven't seen that in a while

**Sam**   I'd punch you

**Noel**   Fucking hell
Charming that is

**Sam**   I'd punch you so hard

**Noel**   Thanks?

**Sam**   For leaving me
I'd punch you for leaving me here
I'd punch you for leaving me here on my own

What is this?
What am I supposed to do with this?

**Noel**   You don't have to do anything
Stop overthinking

It's me
Do whatever you want

---

*4:27pm. 12 November 2021. One month after.*

**Sam** *takes out the same keys from the moment.*

*He clutches them tightly. Kisses his hand.*

**Sam**   I love you I love you I love you I love you

---

**Noel**   Because I knew you would react like this

**Sam**   Okay

**Noel**   I can see now it was –

**Sam**   Stupid?

**Noel**   I didn't think

**Sam**   Deceitful?

**Noel**   I wasn't thinking

**Sam**   Betrayal?

**Noel**    I'm going to give you some time
To
To calm down
Alright?

**Sam**    I am calm don't tell me I'm not calm I'm perfectly calm

**Noel**

**Sam**    I do want you to be honest though

**Noel**

**Sam**    This isn't
We're gay men
Stuff happens I'm not
I don't own you I get it

**Noel**    You're ridiculous

**Sam**    I'm being perfectly rational

**Noel**    You're jealous

**Sam**    I'm
I'm trying to understand why you lied
And if you did something you
Shouldn't
Now is your chance / to say –

**Noel**    Go on keep talking to yourself

**Sam**    You don't care do you?
You don't care that you lied

**Noel**    What do you want me to say?

**Sam**    I want you to say sorry
I want you to say you won't do it again

**Noel**    But I will do it again
It's what friends do

**Sam**    Are you serious?

**Noel**    Matt's mum died
He's in pieces

**Sam**    Don't do that
That isn't the issue

**Noel**    He doesn't have anyone else
He needed someone with him

**Sam**    Take a fucking friend
Not your ex
On your arm
Parading

**Noel**    There you go
There it is

**Sam**    Everyone thinking you're back together
It's horrible

**Noel**    Fuck me you can be so
So heartless sometimes

**Sam**    I'm not heartless I'm insecure
You were with Matt for
For half a decade
It's hard to compete with that

**Noel**    No one is asking you to compete
He's an ex for a reason
There's nothing there

**Sam**    Why did you lie then?
He clearly wants you

**Noel**    Your age is showing, Sam

**Sam**    Did you fuck him?
Just be honest

**Noel**    At his mum's funeral?

**Sam**    Did you fuck him?

**Noel**    You're embarrassing yourself

**Sam**   Answer the fucking question

**Noel**   Are you actively trying to destroy our relationship?

**Sam**   You're the one who won't engage in a conversation
Who gallivants off with his ex in secret

**Noel**   One day when
God forbid
Your mum dies
You'll understand

**Sam**   That's nice isn't it?
Wishing death on my mum/ like that

**Noel**   I'm not wishing death on your mum or anyone

It's the truth
You have to admit you do lack a certain maturity level

**Sam**   Good 'cause if it's gonna be anyone I hope it's you
I hope it's you how about that?

---

**Noel**   You're punishing yourself

**Sam**   Holy –

**Noel**   You're replaying our worst moments

**Sam**   I've lost it
Gone completely –

**Noel**   Over and over again –

**Sam**   Doolally

**Noel**   Is this how you want to remember us?
Fighting?

**Sam**   Am I dreaming?

**Noel**   No

**Sam**   I have these dreams

**Noel**   I know

**Sam**   When I touch you you die
Again
I can't take that

**Noel**   Does this look like a dream?

**Sam** *looks at his surroundings.*

**Sam**   It looks
I mean it's you you're there
It's not you as a
Fox
Or some
You're not blue or green
You look like how you should
We look like
How we should look

**Noel**   Exactly
Even your nose is oily
It's just like real life

**Sam**

**Noel**   See
It's not a dream

**Sam**   So this is
Real?

**Noel**   I'm / still –

**Sam**   Don't say it
Don't ever say it

**Noel**   Alright
Got it

This is only as real as you need it to be

Remember when we went to Rio?
When you said –

**Sam**    Of course I do

Why are you asking me that?

**Noel**    Where did we go?

**Sam**    You know where we went

**Noel**    I want you to tell me

**Sam**    We went to the Jesus

**Noel**    I want to take you back there

**Sam**    What's the point?

**Noel**    To the giant Jesus


**Sam**    You blindfolded me

**Noel**    All the way up to the top
On that little train

**Sam**    Stop it
I'm not going there

**Noel**    The trains pulled up
We're walking up to the top

**Sam**    No

**Noel**    I'm holding your hand
Guiding you

**Sam**    Noel

**Sam** *relents and they are now playing out the memory in present time.*

**Sam** *is closing his eyes.*

**Noel**    And open . . .

Now

**Sam** *opens his eyes.*

**Sam**   Jesus Christ

**Noel**   Yep

**Sam**   Christ

**Noel**   The redeemer
To be exact

**Sam**   It's so

**Noel**   Thirty metres

**Sam**   Jesus

**Noel**   There he is

**Noel** *gets down on one knee.* **Sam** *hasn't noticed. He is still in awe of the monument.*

**Sam**   My eyes
The light

**Noel**   Turn around

**Sam**   He had massive arms
Who knew?

**Noel**   Turn around

**Sam**

**Noel**

**Sam**

**Noel**   Say something

**Sam**   Stand up

**Noel**   Oh fuck

**Sam**   Noel

**Noel**    It's a no

**Sam**    It's not a –

**Noel**    Fuck

**Sam**    No
Look at me
Look at me
You've just made me the happiest man alive

**Noel**    So
It's a

**Sam**    No

**Noel**    Oh okay

**Sam**    But I want to spend the rest of my life with you
So that's a yes

**Noel**    Right

**Sam**    But I just
I don't believe in
I don't think we should force ourselves to fit into something
that isn't purpose-built for us

**Noel**    I don't quite
It's a celebration
Of love
Of unity it's not exclusionary

**Sam**    Well let's do that
The celebration
In our own way

The answer is yes
I want to spend every fucking minute with you I want you to
to
Be my everything
Always

But I don't want to do it anyone else's way
I want to do it our way

**Noel**    Blaze our own trail?

**Sam**    Exactly

So yes
If that's your question

I will spend the rest of my life with you

---

*The street.* **Sam** *sees someone. He thinks it's* **Noel**. *He can only see their backs.*

**Sam**

*He approaches them. Grabs their arm. They turn.*

**Sam**    Sorry
So sorry
I

I thought you were someone
Else
Sorry

---

**Sam**

**Noel**    I love it so much

**Sam**

**Noel**    What?

**Sam**    It's very

**Noel**    Beautiful

**Sam**    In its own way

**Noel**   Bright

**Sam**   It's like

It's big

**Noel**   I know right
Look at the space
All this space would be ours
Look at the garden
It's literally my –

**Sam**   Your dream garden
Yes

**Noel**   I love it

**Sam**

**Noel**   So?

**Sam**   The area
It's very

**Noel**   Very?

**Sam**   Regional yummy mummies and their four by fours

**Noel**   It's safe

**Sam**   The kind of families that rescue opulent-looking
Romanian street dogs called Jaspéire

**Noel**   You're having provincial panic

**Sam**   I'm what?

**Noel**   Cambridge is a vibrant city
It's the academic centre of the world

**Sam**   Well some would say –

**Noel**   You said you were happy to make/ the –

**Sam**   I am

**Noel**    This could be ours

**Sam**    Yours

**Noel**    What's mine is yours
All you have to do is sign and your name is next to mine

**Sam**    That wouldn't be fair
I'm happy to be your tenant

**Noel**    A home isn't just about money Sam –

**Sam**    I've said no

**Noel**    Think of the memories we're gonna make

**Sam**

**Noel**    We could fuck there
And there

**Sam**    Noel

**Noel**    Share breakfast there
Fuck there

**Sam**    Noel


You look

**Noel**

**Sam**    Happy


**Noel**    You prefer the flat

**Sam**    It's not my decision to make

**Noel**    By the Cam?

**Sam**    Cam?

**Noel**    The river

**Sam**    The river is cute

**Noel**    We'd outgrow it

**Sam**    Would we?

**Noel**    This is the one


We can get a cat

Serious

**Sam**    You're not

**Noel**    I am
A rescue

**Sam**    Don't do that
You can't tease that

**Noel**    I'm not teasing

**Sam**    Fuckoff

**Noel**    You could get a kitty cat

**Sam**    Well it wouldn't just be mine it would be

**Noel**    Ours


**Sam**    Put an offer in

**Noel**    Really?

**Sam**    You love it here

Do it

Now

---

*4:27pm. 12 April 2022. Six months after.*
**Sam** *takes out the same keys from the moment.*
*He clutches them tightly. Kisses his hand.*

**Sam**  I love you I love you I love you I love you

---

**Sam**  I'm gonna do it

**Noel**  Take a moment

**Sam**  How dare he
How fucking dare –

**Noel**  One
Two
Three –

**Sam**  / Won't take a moment

**Noel**  Four
Five

**Sam**  Gonna jump up

**Noel**  Happy place

**Sam**  Onto the table
Trample / over the –

**Noel**  I am in control / of my body

**Sam**  Packet stuffing

**Noel**  My actions –

**Sam**  Paxo –

**Noel**  I like Paxo –

**Sam**  Dry shit fucking dry chicken

**Noel**  He shouldn't have said it
Yes

**Sam**  Take this fork and ram it

**Noel**  In his arse

**Sam**  What?

**Noel**   Your thoughts

**Sam**   This isn't a joke

**Noel**   It's a fork
What you gonna do?
Prick him to death

**Sam**   I'm gonna fucking launch it
Across this table
Into his eye in his
Through his eyeball fucking pop it down into his
Head into his
Brain

**Noel**   Legolas step aside
Sam has a fork

**Sam**   It's not funny

**Noel**   A little

You're not gonna do it
He's your dad
It's his birthday for fuck sake
Do something else
I don't know
Blow out his candles

**Sam**   He's a fucking idiot

**Noel**   You're right

**Sam**   Look at him

**Noel**   You can't take him seriously fucking hell
This is the same man who insists Adam and Eve were white
because he's seen pictures

**Sam** *laughs.*

See
That got you

**Sam**   It's not funny
I hate him

**Noel**   You love him

**Sam**   He's such a twat

**Noel**   And you love him


**Sam**   You have no idea what this is like
They're all just sat here
Carrying on as if it's nothing

**Noel**   They don't know what to say

**Sam**   They never accepted you
Me
Us
It's
He called you a friend
You weren't my fucking friend

**Noel**   Thanks

**Sam**   It's like our time together didn't exist
That you were some sort of buddy

**Noel**   Sam

**Sam**   'Everything happens for a reason' my arse

**Noel**   Leave

**Sam**   They have no idea what this pain is
So to just
Say that there's a reason

**Noel**   Get up and leave
You don't need to give this your energy

**Sam**   'One door closes another door opens?'
Nothing is pre-determined people shouldn't use fate as a
safety blanket for the harsh fucking truth that any of us can
just die out of nowhere

At any minute
With no reason for it
No reason

**Noel**

**Sam**    There is no fucking reason for what happened to you
No fucking reason

---

**Sam**    I've been reading

**Noel**    Reading

**Sam**    About near-death experiences
NDEs

**Noel**    Why?
You can just ask me

**Sam**

**Noel**

**Sam**    People who literally died for seconds or minutes
And then survived all experienced things like an
An overwhelming sense of peace
And communicating with a being of golden light

**Noel**    You're making it sound so basic
It doesn't happen like that

**Sam**    While they were dead they saw their loved ones there
Friends who had died
In in in
Beautiful landscapes
Fucking trees
Hills
Waterfalls
Whatever they thought of as beautiful

**Noel**    Sam

**Sam**    There's been studies
It's like a science

**Noel**    Stop it

**Sam**    I could see you again

**Noel**    You can see me now

**Sam**    If I die

**Noel**    Sam

**Sam**    I might get to see you again

**Noel**    You will never see me again

**Sam**    Don't say that
You don't know that

**Noel**    Trust me
I would give anything
To have life
To really be with you again
But that's done
It's final
That part of us is –

**Sam**    Don't say it


**Noel**    This is about –

**Sam**    No

**Noel**    Mum

**Sam**    This has nothing to do with that
Don't belittle me
It's not a reaction

**Noel**    Mum trying to sell the house

**Sam**    Stop it
This isn't that

**Noel**   I told you

I wanted you in on the house
A percentage or something just your name on it but you said
no you weren't
Contributing

**Sam**   I live here
I've paid the fucking
Electric
The bills for years
Doesn't that count for anything?


It's not hers to sell

**Noel**   She owns –

**Sam**   I'm not talking about the legalities Noel
I live here
We live here
This is our home


**Noel**   You didn't want to get married
You didn't want to be on the deeds

**Sam**   Because I'm not some bloody
Sugar baby

**Noel**   We could have avoided this situation if you weren't so
proud

**Sam**   We could have avoided this situation if you'd have left
a fucking will


**Noel**   You're not gonna let her are you?

**Sam**   What?

**Noel**   Sell the house
You're not going to / let her

**Sam**   No of course –

**Noel**    It's not even been a year

**Sam**    She wasn't asking to sell it now
She's not even trying to be difficult she just needs money
In the long run
You're

**Noel**    Not there to –

**Sam**    Yes

**Noel**    Do you think she means it?

**Sam**    I don't know she's your mum

**Noel**    It's too soon
She can't
It can't be sold not yet
She's being selfish she can't just sell our house
You can't let her sell our house

**Sam**    Noel
Stop it
She wouldn't

**Noel**    She can't sell it
Our house
It's all you have
Of
Of our little world

**Sam**    Noel

**Noel**    Promise me she won't sell it
Ever

---

*4:27pm. 12 October 2022. One year after.*

**Sam** *takes out the same keys from the moment.*

*He clutches them tightly. Kisses his hand.*

**Sam**    I love you I love you I love you I love you

---

**Noel** *is over* **Sam***'s shoulder.* **Sam** *is talking to someone else.*

**Sam**    When?

**Noel**    Don't listen to him

**Sam**    When did you do it?

**Noel**    Sam

**Sam**    Where did you do it?

**Noel**    This is bullshit

**Sam**    Matt
Tell me when my boyfriend fucked you

**Noel**    He's lying he's
Hurt

**Sam**    How many times?

**Noel**    He wants to hurt you

**Sam**    Or was it just your mum's funeral?

**Noel**    Sam he's confused

**Sam**    Nice

**Noel**    It's not true
I swear

**Sam**    You can leave now

**Noel**    Sam

**Sam**    I'd like you to get the fuck out of my house

---

**Sam**    Did you fuck him?

**Noel**    At his mum's funeral?

**Sam**   Did you fuck him?

**Noel**   You're embarrassing yourself Sam

**Sam**   Answer the question

---

**Sam** *is in the garden. He is stood before a flowered bush.*

**Noel**   Don't do it

**Sam**   Why?
You can't feel anything

**Noel**   You don't know that

**Sam**   Fuck you
You don't get to speak

**Sam** *rips off a flower.*

**Noel**   It hurts

**Sam**   If only

**Sam** *destroys the plant some more.*

**Noel**   Stop it
This is my
This is my fucking garden
This is our fucking garden

**Sam** *continues to destroy the garden.*

STOP IT
STOP IT YOU'RE KILLING ME

**Sam** *is about to tear a huge chunk of the plant apart.*

I'm sorry

Sam

I said I'm sorry

**Sam**   It's fine

**Noel**   I'm sorry alright?

**Sam**   It's fine

**Noel**   It's not fine

It didn't mean anything
It got out of hand it was
It was a pity fuck we were drunk he was in pain

**Sam**   It's fine

**Noel**   Sam I love you

**Sam**

**Noel**   Sam

**Sam**

**Noel**   I do
So much

**Sam**   I hate you

**Noel**   You don't

**Sam**   I do
I hate you

**Noel**   You don't mean that

**Sam**

**Noel**   Come here

**Sam**   DON'T TOUCH ME
YOU CAN'T TOUCH ME

You're not even around to answer for yourself
You're not able to to
Take responsibility for your actions
To be hated by all our friends for what you did

**Noel**   I'm sorry

**Sam**   I hate you I bloody
Hate / you

**Noel**   Hold me to account

There's nothing I can say
Nothing I can do I know that but –

**Sam**   Why did you do it?

**Noel**

**Sam**   Why did you shame me for guessing the truth?
I was right
And you made me feel like a jealous child

**Noel**   I was scared of / losing –

**Sam**   It's like my my my
Grief
Isn't real now
People
People will look at me/ and think –

**Noel**   / No they won't –

**Sam**   That they can't have been that close that in love
because his boyfriend fucking cheated on him

**Noel**   Let them think it
We know that's bullshit

**Sam**   Do we?

**Noel**   Yes

**Sam**   I don't
I don't know anything anymore

I can't even ask you

**Noel**   Why are you so eager to dismiss me?
Dismiss that I'm real?

**Sam**   Because you're not

**Noel**    You just asked me
And I answered you

**Sam**    You're not real

**Noel**    Aren't I?

**Sam**    You're me
You're my invention
My Frankenstein
I'm in total control of / this experiment

**Noel**    Then why can I say things you don't want to hear?

**Sam**    Intrusive thoughts
It's

**Noel**    You're not in control of my impulses
You're not in control of anything

**Sam**    You're dead Noel

**Noel**    Don't say that
Don't/ ever say –

**Sam**    Because you drowned when your car was –

**Noel**    No no / no no

**Sam**    Smashed into the Cam
You tried to get out you tried but the car it
You had to wait until it was
Submerged
You held your breath

**Noel**    You don't know that?

**Sam**    You didn't want to let it in
Let the water in

**Noel**    You can't know that?

**Sam**    And when you finally kicked out the window it was
too late you couldn't hold your breath anymore –

**Noel**    NO

**Noel** *is completely destroyed by* **Sam**. *He is distraught.*

**Sam**   I need some space

**Noel**   Space?
What do you mean space?

You have all the space you need

I still love you
So much

**Sam**

**Noel**   I miss you
You have no idea

**Sam**

**Noel**   You're never going to see me ag –

---

**Sam**   Hi

**Christian**   Hi

**Sam**   What do you think?

**Christian**   What do I think?

**Sam**   Do you like it?

**Christian**   Um
Do I like it?

I'm not sure
I'm still working it out

What about you
Do you
Like
it?

**Sam**   You're saying that weirdly

**Christian**   No

**Sam**   Like I've done something wrong

**Christian**   You haven't I'm just
Asking you the same question


**Sam**   I mean

Yeah
It's
Hot

**Christian**   Hot?

Is that how it makes you feel?

**Sam**   Oh
Was that what I was meant to ask
How does this piece make you feel?

**Christian**   Maybe

**Sam**   I don't go to many of these things

**Christian**   Neither do I
Thank god

How does it make you feel
If it's hot?

**Sam**   Well
If I think it's hot

It's hot what do you want me to say?

**Christian**   So you feel?

You don't have to blush

**Sam**   I'm not blushing

It makes me feel aroused
I guess

If I find something
If you think something's hot
It's arousing
I'm aroused


It's your picture isn't it?

**Christian**   Yes

**Sam**   Well shit


It's intriguing
It offers depth


I like your work

---

**Noel**   Is this supposed to make us even?

**Sam**

**Noel**   You're sick
Like we haven't suffered enough


He isn't enjoying that

**Sam**

**Noel**   That's our thing
I taught you that
It's ours
He doesn't like it
He didn't even blink

**Sam**

**Noel**   You're wishing it was me

**Sam**   No

**Noel**   Why am I here then?

**Sam**

**Noel**   You're not enjoying it

**Sam**   I am

**Noel**   See there
He got you with his teeth

**Sam**   He didn't

**Noel**   You winced

**Sam**   With pleasure

**Noel**   With pain

You can pretend it's me?

**Sam**   No

**Noel**   Make-up sex
Angry make-up sex

**Sam**   Fuckoff

**Noel** *reaches out to* **Sam**.

GET AWAY FROM ME

**Noel**   Oops
Yeah
We won't be seeing him again

---

*4:27pm. 12 October 2023. Two years after.*

**Sam** *takes out the same keys from the moment.*

*He clutches them tightly. Kisses his hand.*

**Sam**    I love you I love you I love you I love you

---

**Sam**    Happy Birthday

**Noel**    You shouldn't have

**Sam**    I know

I'm sorry

**Noel**    You idiot
You don't need to be sorry

**Sam**    Yes I do

It doesn't matter
You and Matt
It doesn't matter

**Noel**    It does

**Sam**    It does
And it doesn't

I love you and
I know you loved me

**Noel**    Love

**Sam**    Love

I miss you

**Noel**    Course you do

**Sam**    Idiot

**Noel**    Stop it
Stop being sad

**Sam**    I love you

**Sam**    Urgh
It's not fucking working

**Noel**    What have you done to it?

**Sam**    I begged you for a gardener why didn't we get a gardener

**Noel**    I enjoyed it

**Sam**    It's dull

**Noel**    It's relaxing

**Sam**    It's boring

**Noel**    It's being at one with nature

**Sam**    It's not being at one with nature Noel it's mowing a fucking lawn

I'm leaving it

**Noel**    You're not leaving my garden like this

**Sam**    Let it grow let nature take its bloody
Course
Let the plants run free

**Noel**    Is it plugged in?

**Sam**

**Noel**    Well is it?

**Sam**    Yes Noel it's plugged in

I don't know how to do this

**Noel**    Check the oil

**Sam**    It's not a car
It doesn't need

**Noel**    Maybe it does?

**Sam**    Maybe it does

**Noel**    Check the shed

Why are there so many cobwebs?

**Sam**    Because there are spiders

**Noel**    You've ruined my shed

**Sam**    You've ruined my life


WHY ARE THERE SO MANY OILS?

What do you use these for?
Lube?

**Noel**    Focus

**Sam**    Were you fracking?

**Noel**    I tried to teach you once

**Sam**    When you went away

**Noel**    Yes

**Sam**    Stroking
I had to remember it like
Like a cat
Stroke the cat twice
Two stroke

**Noel**    That's a really weird way to
I don't even know what to say to that

**Sam**    Got it

**Noel**    There it is

**Sam**    Fuck yes
I'm a boss

**Noel**    You are

**Sam**    It's going in

**Noel**    If you're wrong you're fucked

**Sam**   Will it blow up?

**Noel**   Maybe

**Sam**   Shit

**Noel**   Here's goes nothing

**Sam**   I'm scared

**Noel**   What's life without risk?


**Sam**   She's alive

**Noel**   Well done baby

**Sam**   I fucking love me

---

**Noel**   I don't pay people to date me

**Sam**   I don't suppose you do

You want to date me?

**Noel**   I'd like to take you on a date

Would you like to go on a date?

---

**Sam**   Did you actually say that?

**Noel**   Sorry?

**Sam**   Would you like to go on a date?
Did you actually say the words?

**Noel**   You know I did

**Sam**   I can't remember if you said that
Or if it was just
You'd like to take me on a date

**Noel**   Does it matter?

**Sam**   I can hear both
I can see both
I
I don't want to forget
I don't want to forget anything

**Noel**   Sam it's just words

**Sam**   Please


**Noel**   I did
You had it right the first time
I did ask

**Sam**

**Noel**   You don't seem convinced

**Sam**

**Noel**   Why don't you believe me?
I'm telling you I said that

**Sam**   Say that again

**Noel**

**Sam**   No
Say that again

**Noel**   What bit?

**Sam**   Say it

**Noel**   Why don't you believe me?
I'm telling you I said that

**Sam**

**Noel**   What?

**Sam**   You sound different you sound

Say something

Now

**Noel**    Okay
Um
I'm not sure what exactly it is you want me to say but I'll just keep talking until you tell / me to –

**Sam**    Your voice
I don't know if it's right

**Noel**    Sam it's me
This is my voice

**Sam**    It's not your voice is
Lower it's

I've forgotten
I'm
Forgetting

**Noel**    You're not

**Sam**    What kind of
Person
Forgets their boyfriend's voice?

**Noel**    I'm here
You see me

**Sam**    You're getting further and further away

**Noel**    Watch a video
Go and watch a video

**Sam**    No

**Noel**    In Rio
On the beach
The dog and the frisbee

**Sam**    I don't want to watch a video
Okay?
The more videos I watch the more memories I lose
Like

Like my brain only has a certain amount of storage of
It's like the more videos I watch the more memories of you
are overwritten with memories of videos
It's all I can see
You can't become a memory of a video

**Noel**

**Sam**   I shouldn't need to watch a video
I should just remember

**Noel**   Sam
Go and watch it

---

**Noel** *is silhouetted centre stage.* **Sam** *is watching on.*

*We hear a large crash. The sound of metal crumpling under intense impact. We hear a splashing sound. The sound of water overwhelms our senses. We are submerged.*

**Noel***'s limbs start to move abstractly. His limbs are heavy, as if moving through thick, heavy water. He is reaching above – as if reaching for the surface.*

*We hear banging on glass. The banging quickens. Becomes harder. More desperate.*

---

**Christian**   You're on a ten-minute veto

**Sam**   Am I?

**Christian**

**Sam**   You're serious?

**Christian**   Deadly

**Christian**   First you tell me to fuckoff
Then you leave me on read
For months

Three months
Block me
More months
Then U-turn
Unblock me
And you ask me out for dinner


**Sam**    I
Um


**Noel**    He wants you to apologise

**Sam**    No
I'm trying to
You can't be here
I'm really trying to

**Noel**    I'm not here to fuck anything up

**Sam**

**Noel**    I'm not
Trust me and roll with me
Okay?

**Sam**

**Noel**    Apologise

**Sam**

**Noel**    Now
He's not joking
He will stand up in a minute and leave your boring ass
unless you tell him that you're sorry and that you're an
arsehole


**Sam**    I'm sorry

I owe an apology
I've been a complete
Arsehole
A fucking weird
Arsehole and I have no fucking idea why you're even here
But thank you

**Noel**   And you want to start again

**Sam**   I just
I thought you were cool

**Christian**   Cool?

**Sam**   You take photos for a living of course you're cool

**Noel**   Nice

**Sam**   Anyway I thought you were
Cool
Or whatever
But I wasn't in a good place and I didn't know how to
compartmentalise thinking that someone was

**Christian**   Cool

**Sam**   Yes
And so time has passed and I'm ready to find someone

**Christian**   Cool

**Sam**   Yes

**Noel**   Are you?

**Sam**   And I can't stop thinking about you
About you and me
About us

**Noel**   You need to be sure

**Sam**   So I asked you here because I think it'd be good to
just

**Noel**    He's a person he feels things too he can't be an experiment

**Sam**    Start again
I'd like to start again

**Christian**    Okay
I can do that

I'm Christian

**Sam**    Sam

---

*4:35pm. 12 October 2024. Three years after.*

**Sam** *takes out the same keys from the moment.*

*He clutches them tightly. Kisses his hand.*

**Sam**    I love you I love you I love you I love you

---

**Noel**    You did it

**Sam**    I did it
Finally
I officially have a degree

**Noel**    Samuel Evert first class honours

**Sam**    Well
Two one but

**Noel**    It was close

**Sam**    It was

**Noel**    Nice mortarboard

**Sam**   Piss
Off

**Noel**   I really appreciated the way it covered your eyebrows

**Sam**   It's not funny it was bloody huge
Someone must have picked mine up by mistake

**Noel**   You probably gave them the wrong measurements

**Sam**   Shut up

**Noel**   Inches not centimetres

**Sam**   They asked for inches actually

**Noel**   Maybe you did it deliberately
Maybe you wanted an abstract beret

**Sam**   If I still had it I would Oddjob you right now

**Noel**   Really?

**Sam**   *GoldenEye* PS Two style
Slice your bloody head off

**Noel**   Charming


**Sam**   You should have been with me

**Noel**   I was
I am

**Sam**   Yeah


**Noel**   Nice of Mum to come

**Sam**   She doesn't age one bit you know

People used to think she was your sister

**Noel**   Younger sister

**Sam**   Right

**Noel**   Christian looks good
You're right he is
Cool

**Sam**   He's young

**Noel**   He's your age
And he likes you

You should introduce him to Mum

**Sam**   I have

**Noel**   Just friends?

**Sam**   Gay men can be just friends Noel

**Noel**   She wasn't born yesterday
She saw the way he looked at you when you were up there
That was a very enthusiastic whoop

**Sam**   It wasn't that loud

**Noel**   Very enthusiastic

**Sam**

**Noel**   She also saw the way you looked at him
You forget
She recognises that look
She's seen it on you before

**Sam**

**Noel**   She won't mind
She doesn't mind
She's happy / for you –

**Sam**   Stop it please

**Noel**   No time like / the present

**Sam**   I said stop

**Noel**    Someone needs to tell you
You can't keep me
My family to one side like we're some / secret

**Sam**    You're not a secret
He knows about –

**Noel**    And expect to share a whole and honest life with someone else
It's not sustainable

**Sam**    I'll do it in my own time
Okay?
When I'm ready
One step at a time
Please


I wouldn't even be here if it wasn't for you

**Noel**    You would
You just needed a push

**Sam**    Or shove

**Noel**    Big shove


Well come on then

**Sam**    Thank you

**Noel**    You're welcome

___

**Sam**    I'm sorry

**Christian**

**Sam**    It's not deliberate I just

**Christian**    Didn't mention it?

**Sam**   Yeah

**Christian**   Right


**Sam**   Say something
I'm going to be late

**Christian**   What do you want me to say?

**Sam**   I don't know but I can't leave on this
Silence
That's not fair

**Christian**   So you can lie but I'm not allowed/ to be silent?

**Sam**   I didn't lie I

**Christian**   You've lied


**Sam**   This is a process Christian it's not like an ex it's not something
Someone I can just be over

**Christian**   I never said it was


I could go with you
Or if it's too soon for that now maybe one day
You need to at least be able to tell me you're seeing his mum

**Sam**

**Christian**   She likes
You said she likes me

**Sam**   She does

**Christian**   So what's the issue?

You're going round for dinner right?

**Sam**   Yeah

**Christian**   It's not some special
Occasion
Day I'm not –

**Sam**   No

**Christian**   So what's the issue?
Why are you excluding me
Hiding seeing her from me

**Sam**

**Christian**   If you said it's a process and it's not something
you can be over you have to let me be part of that process
Share it with me

**Sam**   Okay

**Christian**   I'm not threatened by Noel if that's / what you
think

**Sam**

**Christian**   What?

**Sam**   You just
You don't usually say his name
It's just a bit
Sorry


**Christian**   It's fine
Come here

I'll give you a lift

**Sam**   What?

**Christian**   You're late I've made you late
I'll give you a lift

**Sam**   No

**Christian**   Don't be like that
I said it's fine

If I take you you can have a drink
It'll be nice for you –

**Sam**    No
I don't want you to give me a lift

**Christian**    Okay

Why?

**Sam**    Because that's dangerous that's
This has nothing to do with you
I don't need you to give me a lift

**Christian**    I never said you needed –

**Sam**    You're willing to to
To put yourself on the road for me for no reason
You don't know what could happen
You can't just run around after me I don't need anyone
running around after me

**Christian**    I know
Sam

**Sam**    I'm not a child I don't need a keeper I can drive
myself

**Christian**    Alright


**Sam**    You can't just let me
Do whatever I want
You can't do that

**Christian**    I don't

**Sam**    You can't do that
Promise me you will never do that

---

*4:27pm. 12 October 2025. Four years after.*

**Sam** *is in a different position to what he usually is.*

**Sam**    Fuck

No no no no no

**Sam** *searches his pockets. The keys aren't there.*

Fuck

Fuck

---

The answer is yes
I want to spend every fucking minute with you I want you to
to
Be my everything
Always

---

**Noel**    That's my chair

**Sam**

**Noel**    Sam

Sam you can't throw it out
Tell Chris you're taking it

**Sam**

**Noel**    Sam

**Sam**

**Christian**    Sam can I have a hand please?
It's heavy

**Sam**

**Noel**    Sam you can't just throw it out
That is my fucking chair

**Sam**

**Christian**   Sam

**Sam**

**Noel**   Tell him you're taking it with you

**Sam**

**Christian**   Are you listening?
Hello

**Sam**   Sorry
Here

**Noel**   I can't believe you
You're so
Cold
You're a fucking monster

**Sam**

**Noel**   You never speak to me anymore

**Sam**   I'm sorry

**Noel**   You never hear me

I've been here for you whilst you've
Struggled
Crumbled
I've taken a battering from you
Then you allow Mum to casually sell my house and you
You throw out my things
And you don't even think of me?
Don't / even

**Sam**   / Of course I'm thinking –

**Noel**   Pop me up for one / second to say –

**Sam**   You're here / now

**Noel**   Bye
Let me say bye to our house?

So you do love him?

**Sam**   Yes

**Noel**   And you don't love me anymore?

**Sam**   I'll never stop loving you

**Christian**   Any of this you want to keep?

**Sam**   Um

**Christian**   Speak now or forever hold your peace

**Sam**   It's fine
I've got everything I want

**Noel**   You're burying my life
Our life together

**Sam**   That's not true

**Noel**   Mum's not happy

**Sam**   She gave me her / bless

**Noel**   And you really think she meant that?
She just needs the money
She fucking hates him
The cunt


**Christian**   That's it

**Sam**   Yep

**Christian**   Do you need a
Moment
Or

**Sam**   I don't know

**Noel**   Where is it?

**Sam**   Why am I doing this to myself?

**Noel**    Your new flat
Where is it?

**Sam**    I know it's not you

**Noel**    I want you to say it
Go on

**Sam**    It's by the –

**Noel**    by the fucking river?

**Sam**    Yes

**Noel**    The Cam?
Where I died?

**Sam**    You didn't die in that/ spot –

**Noel**    And you can live with that?
Seeing that every day?
Can you?

It's one of the / flats we –

**Sam**    It's not

**Noel**    Viewed together
Swanky fucking –

**Sam**    It's in the same block
But it's not the
It's not the same

**Noel**    Does Chrissy love it?
Exposed steel beams
Brick walls
Trendy anthracite grey minimalism

**Sam**

**Noel**    Hipster cunt bullshit

**Sam**    You wouldn't be doing this

**Christian**    It's fine if you want a moment Sam
I get it

**Sam**    I'm fine

**Noel**    How would you know?

**Sam**    You would be happy
You have been happy

**Noel**    Happy that you're forgetting
Forgetting my voice
Selling my house/
Erasing our lives –

**Sam**    Please

Please

I don't know if I can do this

**Christian**    What?

**Sam**    It's too much
This is too much

**Christian**    What is?

**Sam**    This
All of this

**Noel**    Actually I'm proud of you

**Sam**

**Noel**    I'm not angry that was you
I'm so proud of you

I'll always be happy for you

Sam
Eh

Come here

**Sam**    I don't know what you would say

**Noel**    Come here

**Sam**    I don't know if I can do this anymore

**Christian**    Do what?

**Sam**    This isn't sane

**Noel**    What is sane?

It isn't a choice
Me or him it isn't
I'm fact I happened
We loved each other
Love
And I died
I'm not here anymore
It doesn't have to be a competition

**Sam**

**Noel**    I'm only here to help you

This is you
You created me
You can't just
Delete me

You want to kill me

**Sam**    No

**Christian**    That's what you're saying
You want to end it

**Sam**    No

**Christian**    All this time
For nothing

**Sam**    That's not what I'm saying

**Noel**    Kill me off/ again –

**Sam**   DON'T SAY THAT

**Christian**   WELL WHAT DO YOU WANT SAM?

**Sam**   To say sorry
I want to say sorry


Every month after
Year
On the day
The twelfth
Four twenty-seven I
I'd stand there with the keys I kept because I somehow
thought that I could could
Take it back
Take all of it back
My giving you the keys
Making you drive / to the –

**Noel**   Stop it

**Sam**   I thought I could take back what I did to you

**Christian**   Stop doing this to yourself

**Sam**   I've never said sorry
Because saying sorry
It
It
It makes it real
What I did and
Admitting

**Noel**   I volunteered

**Sam**   I manipulated you
I wanted you to offer

**Noel**   And I knew that's what you were doing

**Sam**

**Noel**   You needed me to drive ten minutes down the road
and drop off some keys to help you out

**Sam**   So fucking
Selfish
And
Spoilt

**Christian**   That's wasn't much to ask Sam

**Sam**   I didn't know
I didn't how could I
The only bit of the road
The one bit of road
He could have hit you anywhere else and you wouldn't have
gone in
You wouldn't have rolled in

**Noel**   Sam

**Sam**   I'm sorry
I'm so sorry
I'm so so sorry

**Noel**   I love you
And it's okay
All of this is okay
I'm not going anywhere
Yes?

**Sam**   Yes

**Christian**   Because your time
Your time with Noel that's
Untouchable

**Sam**   I know

**Noel**   And selling this place
Filling new time with someone else that doesn't
That doesn't take away from what we shared
You aren't saying goodbye to that

You couldn't say goodbye to that even if you tried
I love you so much

**Sam**  I'm scared
I don't know what to do

**Noel**  I'm not going anywhere
Ever
I'm here 'til your last second
No matter what house
Shit swanky flat
Wherever
I'm here whether you like it or not
I'm here whenever you need me

**Christian**  Are you coming with me?
You don't have –

**Sam**  No
I am tomorrow I just
Can I have tonight?

**Christian**  Of course

**Sam**  It's just tonight

**Christian**  I know

**Sam**  I promise

**Noel**  Sam

**Sam**  It's our last night here
It should just be the two of us

---

*4:27pm. 12 October 2026. Five years after.*

**Sam** *is at peace. He gives* **Noel** *the keys.*

---

**Sam**  I made it

**Noel**    About to be a married man

Just like that your life is over

**Sam**    It's a civil partnership

**Noel**    Yes yes
It's different

You ready?

**Sam**    Ready as I'll ever be

**Noel**    You look beautiful

**Sam**    Happy birthday babe

**Noel**    Thank you

**Sam**    I miss you

**Noel**    She looks so peaceful

**Sam**    Look after her

**Noel**    I will

**Sam**    She was perfect
Every bit the mum I wish I had

**Noel**    Congratulations
Ten years that's
That's really something

**Sam**    Do you think we would have made it this long?

**Noel**    We have

**Sam**    Can you believe it?

**Noel**    She's beautiful
So tiny

**Sam**    What if she doesn't like me?
When she grows up

**Noel**    You'll be a wonderful dad

**Sam**    Christian will be

**Noel**    You both will

**Sam**    Thank you
And don't say it

**Noel**    I haven't –

**Sam**    Don't –

**Noel**    Very straight

**Sam**    Noel!

**Noel**    Breathe

**Sam**    I couldn't cope
Not again

**Noel**    Chris is in good hands
There's so much they can do

**Sam**    I can't do it
Not again

**Noel**    Breathe

**Sam**    Happy birthday dear Christian
Happy birthday to you

**Noel**    A full recovery

**Sam**    For now
He's in remission

**Noel**    That's good

**Sam**    I thought of you

**Noel**    I know

**Sam**    Where did the time go?

**Noel**    She's as stubborn as you are

**Sam**    I'm so proud of her

**Noel**   We all are
She's a beautiful intelligent woman

**Sam**   Graduating first class

**Noel**   Just like her dad

**Sam**   Fuck you

**Noel**   Happy retirement grandaddy

**Sam**   Ha-ha

**Noel**   It looks good on you

**Sam**   You haven't aged a day

**Noel**   That's because / I'm –

**Sam**   You left
You just
Left

**Noel**   Sam

**Sam**   Where did you go?

**Noel**   I died Sam

**Sam**

**Noel**   A long time ago

**Sam**   Do I know you?

**Noel**   Sam
I'm so sorry

**Sam**   I remember your mum
She used to say
If ever I get like that
Take me out
Take me out into the garden and just
Shoot me

**Noel**   I love you

**Sam**   What's it like?
At the end
Does it hurt?

**Noel**   I'm so proud of you

**Sam**

**Noel**   You'll be okay
It's okay

**Sam**

**Noel**   I'll see you soon baby

*Blackout.*

*End.*